T
LittI

ℛ
RAVETTE PUBLISHING

ISBN: 978-1-84161-292-8

This edition first published in 2007 by
Ravette Publishing Limited
Unit 3, Tristar Centre, Star Road,
Partridge Green, West Sussex RH13 8RA
United Kingdom

Written by Gordon Volke

INTRODUCTION

It's A Bloke Thing

Years ago, the wives and girlfriends of keen rugby players or watchers were known as "grass widows". The name implied aching female loneliness caused by male devotion to sport.

But it's not like that nowadays, is it girls? You've caught up now, haven't you?

Or have you?

Nothing like as many women play rugby as play football and the majority of spectators at professional rugby matches are still men. So maybe there's still some way to go in the very blokey world of rugby.

The Rugby-WAGs Training Course

The solution to this problem comes in the shape of this priceless little book.

Here is the game plan ...

1.   You feel shut out from the rugby part of your partner's life. So you want to find out more about the game in order to share his passion.

2. You can't face the idea of trawling through a load of boring rugby books full of technical terms and soppy little diagrams. You want something quick and easy, like a take-away meal.

3. You also want a good laugh along the way.

All you have to do to achieve these goals is to follow, step-by-step, the simple training programme that unfolds here.

Programme Notes

Here's what's on offer. You will be led, in a witty and waggish way, through the mysteries of the two opposing types of rugby with a bit of history thrown in along the way. Then there's some info about how the game is played, the positions on the field and the rules you need to know (all the basic stuff told in an even more basic way). Following that, you'll find a vital resource for any would-be Rugby-WAG ... a run-down, in alphabetical order, of all the rugby terms and jargon used by players and commentators. (You've no idea how many laughs are to be had with that!) Finally, there are some hilarious rugby bloopers, quotable quotes and tasteful rugby jokes ... and *lots* more.

But, first, a glimpse of the sexist world you're entering and the sort of thing you're up against.

RUGBY SONGS

The Captain's Name Was Carter
(By God he was a f**ter!)

Rugby players reveal their true, male chauvinist selves by the songs they sing in the clubhouse after about fifteen pints.

Here's a small selection of the more printable ones. The rude words have been suitably asterisked - not because it avoids any offence, but because it makes them even ruder when you fill in the gaps yourself.

Why was he born so beautiful?
Why was he born at all?
He's no f**king use to anyone,
He's no f**king use at all!

Do your b***s hang low?
Do they dangle to and fro?
Can you tie them in a knot?
Can you tie them in a bow?
Can you sling 'em o'er your shoulder?
Like a continental soldier,
Do your b***s hang low?
Do your b***s hang low?

There was a ram of Derbyshire
That had two horns of brass,
One grew out of its head, sir,
The other grew out of its a*s*.

I know a bear that you all know,
Yogi, Yogi,
I know a bear that you all know,
Yogi, Yogi Bear.

Yogi's got a girlfriend, Suzi,
Suzi, Suzi Bear.

Yogi's d**k is long and green,
Cucum, Cucumber,
Suzi likes to shave her p*b*s,
Grizzly, grizzly bare.

I used to work in Chicago,
At an old department store.
I used to work in Chicago,
But I don't work there any more.

A lady came in for some paper,
Some paper from the store,
Paper she wanted, a ream she got,
I don't work there any more.

Carpet she wanted, shag she got,
Nail she wanted, screw she got,
Fishing rod she wanted, my pole she got,
Meat she wanted, sausage she got,
Beef she wanted, pork she got,
Helicopter she wanted, my chopper she got,
Camel she wanted, hump she got,
F**k she wanted, f**k she got!

And so it goes on. Many little books like this could be filled with these hilarious but essentially caveman lyrics.

They're a good test of your Rugby-WAG potential. If they don't make you smile, you should give up now and take up something like embroidery. But if they blow your whistle, you're a true Rugby-WAG in the making.

Read on, girl. Read on!

HISTORY OF THE GAME

Now Here's The Catch

Everybody knows that the game of rugby originated at Rugby School. But how exactly did it happen?

A plaque on the wall of the school tells the story:

This stone commemorates the exploit of William Webb Ellis, who, with a fine disregard for the rules of football, as played in his time, first took the ball in his arms and ran with it, thus originating the distinctive feature of the rugby game. AD 1823.

What a cocky little git! If he'd done that nowadays at the local Comp, he wouldn't have invented a new game. He would have ended up face-down in the mud with a nice close-up on someone's video phone and the whole thing on the Net within the hour.

Havin' A Ball

Rugby is a game for the mentally deficient. That is why it was invented by the British.

Who else but an Englishman could invent an oval ball?

Peter Pook

Rugby's distinctive oval-shaped ball came into being in the 1850s. Two shoe-makers called *Richard Lindon* and *William Gilbert*, whose workshop was right opposite Rugby School, supplied balls to the boys made from inflated pigs' bladders encased in leather. These bladders tended to be oval or plum-shaped rather than round, so the ball followed that shape. Not until 1892 was the exact shape and size of the ball written into the rules.

Properly called a *prolate-spheroid*, a rugby ball bounces in a way that's almost impossible to predict. This baffles and irritates both teams, driving them to new heights of violence towards each other (which is, after all, the true purpose of the game).

Come On You Blues

Have you ever wondered why so many major sports, football and tennis included, started life properly in the second half of the 19th Century? The answer must be that the Victorians were so sexually repressed, they felt the need to bash the hell out of something (or each other) on a regular and organised basis. Certainly, rugby falls into this category. The Rugby Football Union was formed in 1871 and drew up a set of rules based on the game invented at Rugby School. The first Varsity Match between Oxford and Cambridge took place in 1872.

THE TWO RUGBY CODES

A Code In The Head

There are two different types of rugby. One is called *Rugby Union*. The other is called *Rugby League*.

Rugby Union is what most people call "Rugby". The teams have 15 players each. This type of rugby is the faster version played at public schools, universities and everywhere in Wales.

Rugby League did not come into existence until 1893 and only has 13 players a side. This is the rougher, tougher variant played mainly by professional teams "oop North".

These two different styles of rugby are called *codes*. Often, you hear about professional players *switching codes* to the other type of game - usually because the money is better.

As you might imagine, there's not a great deal of love lost between Rugby Union and Rugby League...

League is much, much more physical than Union, and that's before anyone starts breaking the rules.

Adrian Hadley

This book is about Rugby Union and will go with the convention of just calling it "rugby". According to many car bumper stickers, it's a *game played by men with odd-shaped balls* and a famous old saying has it that *football is a gentleman's game played by hooligans; rugby is a hooligan's game played by gentlemen*.

Whatever the truth of this perceived wisdom, stand by for an accurate definition of the game and then some essential rugby facts.

COMIC DEFINITION OF RUGBY

Nice One, Bertie!

In 1930, comic novelist P.G. Woodhouse described rugby in a way that tells you all you really need to know about the game.

In *Very Good, Jeeves*, Bertie Wooster says:

Rugby football is a game I can't claim absolutely to understand in all its niceties, if you know what I mean. I can follow the broad, general principles, of course. I mean to say, I know that the main scheme is to work the ball down the field somehow and deposit it over the line at the other end and that, in order to squalch this programme, each side is allowed to put in a certain amount of assault and battery and do things to its fellow man which, if done elsewhere, would result in 14 days without the option, coupled with some strong remarks from the Bench.

So there you are. Rugby in a nutshell!

BASICS OF THE GAME

Your Starter For Ten

Here are ten important things about the game that every proper Rugby-WAG should know...

1. Rugby is played on a grass pitch measuring 100 yards by 75 yards. A match lasts 80 minutes.

2. It is essentially a game of running, throwing and catching. If a player drops the ball, this is called a *knock-on* and is a foul.

3. The ball can be kicked forwards, but it can NEVER be thrown forwards. It must always be passed *backwards*. A *forward* pass is always a foul.

4. If the players from one team succeed in touching the ball on the ground behind their opponent's goal line, they score a *try*. This is worth 5 points.

5. A kick at goal is then taken from a point in line with where the try was scored. If the kicker succeeds in booting the ball over the crossbar

and between the tall posts, he *converts* the try and scores a further 2 points.

6. Points can also be scored by two other successful kicks at goal. A *penalty kick*, awarded for foul play by the opposing team, scores 3 points. *A drop-kick*, executed by a player during open play, scores 3 points as well. The team with the most points at the end of the game is the winner.

7. If the ball goes out of play along the side of the pitch, it is called *going into touch*. This results in a *lineout*. The players form a line and jump to catch the ball as it is thrown back into play.

8. When play gets scrappy or some minor infringement has taken place, the referee blows for a *scrum*. This is where some of the players form a weird, circle-shaped huddle and try to push each other over/crush each other to death. The ball is popped into the side of this grunting, groaning human "house" and is

ejected out of the back by one side
or the other, thus giving them
possession and allowing the game to
continue.

9. Players running with the ball can be
    stopped by the other side. This is
    called *tackling*. Usually, the runner's
    legs are grabbed and he is pulled
    down.

10. After a tackle, the ball can go loose
    and the other players gather round,
    trying to get hold of it. Depending
    whether they use their hands or feet

to reach the ball, this is called a *maul* or a *ruck*. There are all sorts of technical rules about both states of play - but don't you bother your pretty little head about them. (Sorry ... slipped into sexist rugby mode for a moment.)

Right! That's it for now. More fun stuff coming up next to avoid info-overload.

FUNNY COMMENTATOR BLOOMERS

Nice TRY!

Rugby is a fast-moving and exciting game. So here's what happens when TV and radio commentators try to describe it to us...

Dusty Hare kicked 19 out of the 17 points.
David Coleman

I don't want to sit on the fence, but it could go either way.

Maurice Banford

If you didn't know him, you wouldn't know who he was.

Nigel Starmer-Smith

That could have made it 10 - 3 and there's a subtle difference between that and 7 - 3.

Bill Maclaren

Of course, they don't play to any sort of pattern and, if you're not careful, you will start playing to that pattern.

Mike Davies

He's like a needle in a haystack, this man he's everywhere.

Ray French

An easy kick for George Fairburn now but, as everybody knows, no kicks are easy.

David Doyle-Davidson

Paul Allot drying the wet ball which is a disadvantage in Lancashire's favour.

Frank Hayes

The Wigan defence allowed him two bites at the shot.

Radio Manchester Commentator

POSITIONS ON THE PITCH

If I Were The Marrying Kind

If I were the marrying kind,
Which thank the Lord I'm not, Sir,
The sort of man that I would wed
Would be a rugby SCRUM-HALF.

He'd put it in and I'd put it in,
We'd both put it in together.
We'd be all right in the middle of the night,
Putting it in together.

Ah! Another timeless classic. To
understand it properly, you need to
know what a scrum half is and what he

does on the field. So here's a quick rundown of all the positions.

Part 1: Forwards (The Pack)

There are 8 of these, most of them great beer-swilling bruisers who collectively weigh more than a double-decker bus.

* The Props
(Tight Head and Loose Head)

Wear shirt Nos 1 and 3

Front row of the scrum. Hard men who lock horns with the opposition like rutting stags.

* The Hooker

Wears shirt No 2

Usually a little chap who is supported by the Props either side. This enables him to "hook" the ball backwards when it's put into the scrum, giving his team possession.

* The Second Row

Wear Nos 4 and 5

Beefier and even more violent than the three in the front row. Do a lot of pushing, supposedly to gain ground but in fact to trample the collapsing opposition to a pulp.

* Flankers (Wing Forwards)

Wear Nos 6 and 7

These guys join the scrum in a half-hearted sort of way on either side. Other than that, nobody quite knows what else they do.

(*Note* - if quoting this item of info in an attempt to raise your Rugby-WAGs-cred, be careful not to get the F of Flankers and the W of Wing muddled up.)

* Number 8 (Lock)

Not surprisingly, wears No 8 shirt.

Bravely sticks his head between the two huge hairy arses of the Second Row forwards, completing the scrum formation and supposedly "locking" it together.

When the Forwards aren't grunting and swearing in the scrum, they lumber around the field trying to catch up with the play. They're known as "The Pack" because they move around together like wolves, but they lack the speed, cunning and almost everything else of their four-footed namesakes.

Part 2: The Backs

There are 7 of these guys, all lightweights who are fast runners, good at dodging about to avoid tackles.

* Scrum-Half

Wears No 9 shirt

This is a specialist position normally filled by someone small and nippy. It's the scrum-half's job to put the ball into the side of the scrum and then collect it when it's hooked out of the back. He also receives the ball when it's knocked down to him at the lineout. On either occasion, he has to throw the ball to the other backs who wait in a line to run with it.

* Stand-Off (Fly Half)

Wears No 10

The player who receives the ball from the scrum-half. Has to decide whether to run with it, pass it down the line or kick it forwards.

* The Centres (The Three-Quarters)

Wear shirt Nos 12 and 13

These two athletic types sprint forward with the ball or run head-first into the opposition (know as the crash ball). It's their job to make ground and try to get near the other side's goal line.

* The Wingers

Wear shirt Nos 11 and 14

Really fast types who dash down either side of the pitch with the ball. Mostly get swatted into touch like flies.

and finally ...

* The Full Back

Another special position right at the back of the team. You must be a good catcher because the opposition often boot the ball down the field towards you and, if you miss it, they go on to score a try.

When the backs are playing well together, it's really exciting to see the ball being passed along the line as they race down the pitch together and score a try.

RUGBY JOKES

It's A Joke Thing

As you'd expect, given the hunting-tribe nature of rugby and the tribesmen who play it, there are lots of good jokes associated with the game.

So take a break and enjoy this little selection. We'll continue your Rugby-WAGs education in the next section.

Why don't rugby players suffer from mid-life crises?
They never get past adolescence.

Why do rugby players like intelligent women?
Opposites attract, don't they?

Rugby player:
Doctor, doctor! When I get up in the morning and look in the mirror, I feel like throwing up. What's wrong with me?

Doctor:
I couldn't say, but there's nothing wrong with your eyesight.

A chap was dancing with a rather snooty partner who was getting increasingly cross with his clumsiness. Having stepped on her toes three times, he said: "I'm terribly sorry. I'm a little stiff from rugby."

"I don't give a shit where you're from," she replied. "I'm not dancing with you any more!"

A woman walked into the Ladies' Room at the rugby club and was horrified to see a man weeing into the toilet.

"Do you mind!" she exclaimed. "This is for women only!"

"So is this!" he replied.

A player with a reputation for being rude to officials went up to the referee who had just made a dubious offside decision.

"What would you do if I called you a stupid prick?" asked the player.

"I'd show you a red card and send you off, of course," replied the ref.

"Supposing," continued the player, "I only thought you were a stupid prick?"

"In that case," murmured the referee, "if you only thought it, I couldn't really do anything."

"In that case," said the player, "I think you're a stupid prick!"

RUGBY TERMS

Terms of Endearment

Rugby players have lots of cute terms for different parts of their game - *like calling for the mark, the 22 and the sin bin*. To find out what they all mean, here's a list of the more common expressions with suitably WAGGISH explanations.

(They're in alphabetical order for easy reference.)

Against The Head

This phrase applies to a scrum. If the scrum-half from one team puts the ball in the side, it is expected that his team will hook it backwards and eject it out of their side of the scrum, so retaining possession. If the opposing team succeeds in getting the ball out of the opposite side of the scrum, that is called *winning the ball against the head*.

Blood Bin

If your best player is punched on the nose in the first minute, you don't necessarily lose him for the rest of the game. He can go and sit in the Blood Bin, a special place where bleeding wounds are treated.

Meanwhile, another player takes the field in his place. When the star player has been suitably patched up, the substitute player comes off and his better can retake the field.

Calling For The Mark

This business can only happen in the area in front of your own goalposts. The opposition have kicked the ball down the field and are charging towards you, intent on mangling you into a jelly. You have three choices -

a) Run off the field shrieking "Mummy!"

b) Catch the ball and kick it back or pass it to a team-mate.

c) Catch the ball and shout "Mark" as you dig one heel into the ground.

If you perform option 3 successfully, you are awarded a free kick from the spot where you made the mark. This has the effect of halting the advance of the snarling hordes.

Drop Kick
The rugby equivalent of a half-volley in tennis. You drop the ball just in front of you and kick it the moment it touches the ground. Used for restarting the game and scoring drop goals.

Feeding (Not Straight)
This prevents the scrum-half giving his groaning forwards and their half-crushed hooker an unfair advantage in the scrum. If the ball is fed to them by rolling it in right under their feet, they can easily hook it backwards and win

possession. So the ref has to see that the ball is put in straight to give both teams an equal chance of winning it.

Fly-Hack

If the ball is bobbing around with nobody near it, you're allowed to boot it up the field and then run after it. Can be a smart move if you gain a lot of ground as a result, but you risk giving the ball straight back to the opposition.

Goose Step

A clever ply to avoid being tackled. You run with your legs high in the air, like a prancing horse.

Jock Strap

This item of sporting attire is worn by sportsmen in all kinds of different sports, so why it should be so closely associated with rugby is something of a mystery. Maybe it's because rugby players are fixated on what it supports.

Kicking For Touch

Touch, you will remember, is the rugby term for the sidelines of the pitch. Sometimes, players deliberately kick the ball downfield so that it goes out of play or into touch.

This is not as silly as it sounds. If the ball does not go out of play, the other side can just pick it up and boot it back.

If it goes into touch, however, everyone has to charge up field to where it went out of play for the lineout. This means you gain a lot of ground and keep it.

Kick Off

The game is started (and restarted after a try has been scored and converted) at the centre spot. The ball is drop-kicked down the field and must reach the opponent's ten metre line (see page 61). The kicking team charge after the ball while their opponents try to catch it before they get flattened.

Late Tackle

This is when a player is tackled after he has got rid of the ball. It's a foul and results in a penalty kick. If the player has got rid of the ball by kicking it upfield, the penalty is taken from where the ball lands, rather than where the late tackle took place. (That's only fair, don't you think?)

Maul

As mentioned earlier, this is a general brawl (usually violent) in which both sides try to get possession of the ball which is not touching the ground. Regulated by all kinds of laws which nobody obeys and the ref doesn't understand, so don't worry about them. If they don't, you needn't.

Offside

Because you are never allowed to pass the ball forwards, you'd think the offside rule in rugby would be clear and simple - if you're in front of the ball, you're offside. Well, that's correct ... and it's not! There are all sorts of weird and wonderful exceptions like not retiring or coming in on the wrong side. DON'T GO THERE! It's a minefield of complexity and confusion that will rapidly drain you of the will to live.

Out-On-The-Full
Change the "F" to a "P" and you'll know
where the players go on a Saturday night
after the pubs close. The phrase itself
means to kick the ball out of play
without it touching the ground.

Place Kick
Any kick that involves placing the ball
on the ground first. (You usually see the
kicker build a little mound and place the
ball on it with extreme care, like
handling a precious ornament.)

Punt
Dropping the ball onto your foot and kicking it before it touches the ground.

Reverse Pass
This is a cunning ploy employed by the backs to confuse the opposition. They pass the ball behind their backs. Works brilliantly well if a team-mate is there to receive it. If not, it looks pretty silly.

Ruck

The same sort of aggressive shoving-match as a maul, only this time the ball is on the ground. Again, all sorts of rules apply. And again, leave well alone.

Scissors Pass

This is another cunning ploy used by the backs. They run across each other's paths, switching the ball, in a criss-cross shape like a pair of scissors.

Sevens

A shortened form of the 15-man game involving 7 players. It's a sort of mini-rugby for grown-ups.

Side Step
A smart way of avoiding an oncoming tackle.

Sin Bin
Rugby copied this idea from ice hockey, another he-man team game with built-in ultra-violence. If you keep breaking the rules, you're shown a *yellow card* and sent off for ten minutes. This means your team has to continue with one man short. If you come back on and continue to misbehave (or do something really dangerous at any time) you get a *red card*. Then you're sent off and not allowed to come back on.

Spin Pass

This means putting a spin on the ball as you throw it which helps it to fly a long distance through the air.

Substitutions

Unlike football, which only allows four subs, rugby allows a total of seven. Apart from visiting the Blood Bin, a player cannot come back onto the field once he has been substituted.

Ten Metre Line
A line across the pitch, ten metres from the centre line. It's a useful point of reference with a variety of uses, the main one being to give the groundsman something to do with his white-lining machine.

Twenty Two Metre Line (usually just known as the 22)
Another line across the pitch, this time 22 metres in front of either goal. This one's important - it's the rugby equivalent of the penalty area in football.

This is "home territory". Alarm bells ring when the opposition reaches your 22. Conversely, unbounded joy and excitement is felt on reaching theirs.

Twenty-Two Metre Drop-Out
No, this isn't some hippie who hangs round the goal area saying "peace, man" to the feuding players. It's a way of restarting the game. If the opposition carry the ball over your goal line but fail to touch it down and score a try, they must give up the ball. Your team can

then line up along the 22 metre line and charge up field as the ball is drop-kicked back into play.

Up-and-Under
A high kick that stays in the air long enough for the kicker (or any of his team-mates who were behind the ball when it was kicked) to charge forwards and catch it again. Used for gaining short distances. More associated with Rugby League than Rugby Union.

Wheeling The Scrum

When the irresistible force of one set of forwards meets the immovable object of the other, all that huffing and grunting energy has to go somewhere - and it often results in the scrum turning round like a wheel. This is not allowed. So the scrum has to be started again.

FUNNY RUGBY QUOTES

A Few More Points Scored

Your Rugby-WAGs training course is two-thirds of the way through and you've worked hard on the previous section. So you deserve a break.

Here are some classic quotes about the game you're coming to love and understand ...

Rugby is a good occasion for keeping thirty bullies from the centre of the city.

Oscar Wilde

*I prefer rugby to soccer ... I enjoy the
violence in rugby, except when they start
biting each other's ears off.*

Elizabeth Taylor

*I think you enjoy the game more if you don't
know the rules. Anyway, you're on the same
wavelength as the referees.*

Jonathan Edwards

*The relationship between the Welsh and
English is based on trust and understanding.
They don't trust us and we don't understand
them.*

Dudley Wood

I may not have been very tall or very athletic, but the one thing I did have was the most effective backside in world rugby.

Jim Glennon

Get your retaliation in first.

Carwyn James

A major rugby tour by the British Isles to New Zealand is a cross between a medieval crusade and a prep school outing.

John Hopkins

England's coach Jack Powell, an immensely successful businessman, has the acerbic wit of Dorothy Parker and, according to most New Zealanders, a similar knowledge of rugby.

Mark Reason

The only hope for the England rugby team is to play it all for laughs. It would pack them in if the public address system at Twickenham was turned up full blast to record the laughs at every inept bit of passing, kicking or tackling. The nation would be in fits ... and, on telly, the BBC

*would not need a commentator but just a
tape of that Laughing Policeman, turning it
loud at the most hilarious bits.*

Jim Rivers

*Colin Meads is the kind of player you expect
to see emerging from a ruck with the remains
of a jockstrap between his teeth.*

Tom O'Reilly

*Forwards are the gnarled and scarred
creatures who have a propensity for running
into and bleeding all over each other.*

Peter Fitzsimmonds

The pub is as much a part of rugby as is the playing field.

John Dickenson

And finally, a variant of the famous quote mentioned earlier:

Rugby is a beastly game played by gentlemen; soccer is a gentleman's game played by beasts and (American) football is a beastly game played by beasts.

Henry Blaha

THE OFFICIALS

Not To Be Dissed

Because of the nature of the game (almost unlimited body contact with little or no padding), the rugby world frowns on unsporting behaviour.

So says the rugby entry in the encyclopaedia.

Yeah, right!

Rugby players, like football players and the entire criminal fraternity, know it's really all about what you can get away with. *(As one convict once remarked to another: You ain't in here for what you did, Johnny. You're in here for getting caught.)* So it's up to the officials to make sure that the rules are obeyed and the lofty ideals of rugby are upheld.

Enter The Old Farts

Many refs are drawn from the ranks of keen ex-players who are known in the rugby world as rugger buggers or old farts. They make good refs because they know all the tricks of the trade and can spot when a player is going to break the rules even before he does. (By the way, the rules of the game are actually called laws, but everyone calls them rules so we will too.) The problem these geriatric refs have, is keeping up with the play. Despite being permanently 40 metres behind the ball, rugby refs rule the game with a rod of iron. Unlike soccer refs, who just blow their whistles occasionally and make the odd hand signal, rugby refs TALK all the time. They engage in a running commentary, explaining their decisions and chastising the players for their misconduct. And the players never answer back. You should never challenge authority directly in a rugby match. You just try to get away with it on the quiet.

Is He Flagging?

The referee is assisted by two linesmen called touch judges.
These guys run up and down the sidelines, indicating when the ball has gone out of play and keeping an eye out for any aggro on the pitch. When a try is scored, they congregate under the posts and wave their flags madly if the kicker

succeeds in converting the try. This is a necessary and useful safeguard because, for some strange reason, it is often hard to tell if the ball has gone over properly despite the posts being the size of a house.

THE COMPETITIONS

Twickers And All That

There are lots of names and places in this section that every good Rugby-WAG should know by heart. So pay attention, please. Questions will be asked later!

Competitive professional rugby is played at three levels - club level and two international levels - the annual "home nations" championships and overseas tours (including the rugby World Cup). Here's a very brief rundown about all of them ...

Club Rugby

This commands nothing like the same
following as club football and is very
seldom televised on any free-to-air
channels. So don't you worry too much
about it yourself.

Suffice to say that if you hear names like
*Wasps, Saracens, Harlequins, Sale, Bath,
Leicester and London Irish* (to name but a
few), you're in the realm of top league
club rugby. The proper name for this is
The Premiership and, at the moment, it
is sponsored by Guinness. (As in
football, there are other divisions below,
so promotion and relegation take place

at the end of each season. No need to bother with any of this either unless you decide to follow the fortunes of your local team.)

The Heineken Cup

This is a knockout competition for the top rugby teams from all over Europe. *Quick joke -*

"My team played a French side in the Heineken Cup."
"Toulouse?"
"No, we won 23 - 15"

Not surprisingly, it's sponsored by

Heineken lager and culminates in the Heineken Cup Final, a very grand occasion that gets televised. (If you're forced to watch it, use it as an opportunity to show off your new-found Rugby-WAG status.)

The Six Nations

England, Scotland, Wales, The Republic of Ireland, France and Italy take part in this annual competition. Usually, there is just a winner, but sometimes this winner beats all the other teams. This is called gaining the *Grand Slam*. The losing team every year gains the *Wooden Spoon*.

Because the home nations annual rugby tournament was scrapped many years ago, these games attract great interest and are overwhelmingly nationalistic. The match between England and Scotland even has its own name, The Calcutta Cup, and is played in a hothouse of patriotism on both sides. The same is true of England v Wales and England v Ireland.

*   *England* play at *Twickenham*, the "home" of rugby. The site in South London was a ten-acre vegetable patch when it was first chosen for

development in 1907. Since then, it has grown out of all recognition and is now a huge modern stadium seating 82,000 people.

* *Scotland* play at *Murrayfield* in Edinburgh. This stadium holds the record for the largest number of people to watch a home nations rugby game - 104,000 in 1975 for Scotland v Wales.

* *Wales* play at *The Millennium Stadium* in Cardiff which replaced the famous *Cardiff Arms Park*. It seats 72,500 people and has a retractable roof.

*   At the moment, *The Republic of Ireland* play at *Croke Park*, the home of Gaelic Football in Dublin. They are waiting for their traditional home, *Lansdowne Road*, to be refurbished.

*   *France* play at the *Stade De France* in Paris and *Italy* play at a tiny ground called the *Stadio Flaminio* in Rome. (That's all you need to know about them. They're foreign.)

The British Lions

It's a funny old world, isn't it? As soccer nations, the home nations will not even countenance the formation of a British team to enter international competitions like the World Cup, even though they rarely manage to qualify for the finals these days (England being the exception - and they don't always find it easy!). Yet in rugby, it's the other way round. Despite all the Jingoism surrounding the national rugby teams, players are drawn from all four home nations to make The British Lions. They often play well together, despite not being able to understand each other's accents.

All Abroad

When the British Lions go on tour, they play the following countries - *Australia, New Zealand, South Africa* and South Seas teams like *Fiji, Western Samoa* and *Tonga*. These teams are all very strong and usually thrash the visitors by an embarrassingly high score - another example of the Mother Country teaching the Dominions a new game and then living to regret it.

The World Cup

The home nations are on their own again for this tournament which takes place every four years. England won the trophy in 2003 with a famous victory over Australia in which Jonny Wilkinson kicked the winning drop-goal in the dying seconds of extra time. Teams from all over the world compete in this one, including *America, Canada, Japan* and *Argentina*.

FUN QUIZ

Exam Time

Are you feeling nervous? Quickly, then! There's just time to nip to the loo before your big test.

When you've answered these fun quiz questions, you'll know whether you've finally made it as a fully-trained Rugby-WAG.

Good Luck!

1. What were early rugby balls made from?

   a) Wood
   b) Pigs' bladders encased in leather
   c) Old underpants stuffed into a sock

2. In rugby, you are allowed to pass the ball forward, but never kick it forward.

   a) True
   b) False

3. Who "ran with the ball" and invented the game of rugby at Rugby School?

   a) William Webb Ellis
   b) Sophie Ellis Bextor
   c) Harry Webb aka Cliff Richard

4. Which home country plays its rugby at Murrayfield?

5. Can you complete this sentence?

   The two different types of rugby - Rugby Union and Rugby League, are called the two - - - - -

6. What is the proper name for the sidelines of a rugby pitch?

a) Sidelines
b) Tramlines
c) Touch

7. Unscramble these letters to spell the name of the strange "huddle" that rugby players form to decide who gains possession of the ball ...

R U M C S

8. Where do players who have committed lots of fouls go to?

   a) The Pub
   b) The Sin Bin
   c) Hell

9. How many points are scored by the following? (You must get *all three* correct to gain a right answer!)

   a) A try
   b) A conversion
   c) A penalty goal or drop-kick goal

10. What is the name of the team, drawn from the four home nations, that goes on overseas rugby tours?

11. A maul and a ruck are both types of general, free-for-all, pushing and shoving matches when the ball goes loose in open play.

    a) True
    b) False

12. What are Wasps, Harlequins and Saracens?

    a) Slang terms for sexually-transmitted diseases
    b) New pop groups
    c) Premiership rugby clubs

13. Who are known as rugger buggers or old farts?

14. Where is the home of English rugby?

    a) Twickenham
    b) Wembley
    c) Milton Keynes

15. What is the group name for the eight rugby forwards?

    a) The Pack
    b) The Pack Animals
    c) The Animals

Answers

1. b) Pigs' bladders are encased in leather
2. b) False (it's the other way round - you can kick the ball forwards, but never pass it)
3. a) William Webb Ellis
4. Scotland
5. Codes
6. c) Touch
7. SCRUM
8. b) The Sin Bin
9. a) A try - 5 points
   b) A conversion - 2 points
   c) A penalty or drop-kick - 3 points
10. The British Lions
11. a) True
12. c) Premiership Rugby Clubs
13. Ex rugby players
14. a) Twickenham
15. a) The Pack

Score Ratings

0 - 5 right:

a Grade C pass. Please revise and re-sit if you wish to improve your Rugby-WAG status.

6 - 10 right:

a Grade B pass. Well done. You know enough to call yourself a Rugby-WAG.

11 - 15 right:

a Grade A pass. Congratulations! You are a clued-up and fully-fledged expert Rugby-WAG.

CONCLUSION

If you didn't score any points through complete lack of interest, here's your get-out clause ...

Don't be a Rugby-WAG ... just be a WAG!

Here's what you do ...

* wear designer clothes and sunglasses
* keep your tan well topped up
* display lots of bling
* never be seen without make-up
* shop 'til you drop
* drive the latest off-roader or sports car
* be seen at the trendiest nightclubs
* use a flashy mobile phone
* be aware of the paparazzi and make sure you have a pose and pout ready for them at all times

Does that sound better?

Then go for it ... if you can afford it!!